DETAINED AND INTERROGATED

ANGEL ISLAND IMMIGRATION

Virginia Loh-Hagan

45TH PARALLEL PRESS

Published in the United States of America by Cherry Lake Publishing
Ann Arbor, Michigan
www.cherrylakepublishing.com

Reading Adviser: Marla Conn, MS, Ed., Literacy specialist, Read-Ability Inc.
Cover Designer: Felicia Macheske

Photo Credits: Photo Credits: © Rommel Canlas/Shutterstock.com, cover, 1; © Library of Congress, LC-USZ62-3976, 5;
© Everett Historical/Shutterstock.com, 6; © pamas/Shutterstock.com, 11; © ChameleonsEye/Shutterstock.com, 12;
7452280/ Department of Treasury. Public Health Service, 17; © 7452281/ Department of Treasury. Public Health
Service, 18; © Courtesy of the California Historical Society, 21; © Library of Congress, LC-DIG-highsm-25213, 22;
© Library of Congress, LC-DIG-highsm-25225, 25; © Library of Congress, LC-DIG-highsm-25218, 29

Graphic Elements Throughout: © Chipmunk131/Shutterstock.com; © Nowik Sylwia/Shutterstock.com;
© Andrey_Popov/Shutterstock.com; © NadzeyaShanchuk/Shutterstock.com; © KathyGold/Shutterstock.com;
© Black creator/Shutterstock.com; © Edvard Molnar/Shutterstock.com; © Elenadesign/Shutterstock.com;
© estherpoon/Shutterstock.com

45th Parallel Press is an imprint of Cherry Lake Publishing.

Library of Congress Cataloging-in-Publication Data
Names: Loh-Hagan, Virginia, author.
Title: Detained and interrogated : Angel Island immigration / by Virginia Loh-Hagan.
Other titles: Detained and interogated
Description: Ann Arbor, Michigan : Cherry Lake Publishing, [2020] | Series:Behind the curtain | Includes index.
Identifiers: LCCN 2019032971 (print) | LCCN 2019032972 (ebook) | ISBN9781534159396 (hardcover) |
    ISBN 9781534161696 (paperback) | ISBN9781534162846 (ebook)
Subjects: LCSH: Angel Island Immigration Station (Calif.)—Juvenileliterature. | San Francisco Bay Area (Calif.)—
    History—Juvenileliterature. | Chinese—United States—Juvenile literature. | Immigrants—United States—Juvenile
    literature. | UnitedStates—Emigration and immigration—History—Juvenile literature. | China—Emigration and
    immigration—History—Juvenile literature. | Readers' theater.
Classification: LCC JV6926.A65 L64 2020 (print) | LCC JV6926.A65 (ebook) | DDC 304.8/73—dc23
LC record available at https://lccn.loc.gov/2019032971
LC ebook record available at https://lccn.loc.gov/2019032972

Cherry Lake Publishing would like to acknowledge the work of the Partnership for 21st Century Learning,
a Network of Battelle for Kids. Please visit *http://www.battelleforkids.org/networks/p21* for more information.

Printed in the United States of America
Corporate Graphics

A Note on Dramatic Retellings

Participating in Readers Theater, or dramatic retellings, can greatly improve reading skills, especially fluency. The books in the **BEHIND THE CURTAIN** series give readers opportunities to learn about important historical events in a fun and engaging way. These books serve as a bridge to more complex texts. All the characters are real figures from history; however, their stories have been fictionalized. To learn more about the people and the events, check out the Viewpoints and Perspectives series and the Perspectives Library series, as the **BEHIND THE CURTAIN** books are aligned to these stories.

TABLE of CONTENTS

HiSTORICAL
BACKGROUND

In the early 1900s, many immigrants went through the Angel Island Immigration Station. They were processed there. Government officials decided whether or not they could enter the United States.

There were many different immigrant groups at Angel Island. There were Australians, Russians, and Asians. But one group was treated differently. Chinese immigrants were targeted.

U.S. workers were threatened by Chinese workers. They thought Chinese workers were taking their jobs. In 1882, the Chinese Exclusion Act was passed. This law banned Chinese laborers from immigrating. This was the first time the United States excluded a specific cultural group. Only Chinese people who worked skilled jobs were allowed to immigrate. They could even bring their family from China.

FLASH FACT!

President Chester A. Arthur signed the Chinese Exclusion Act.

Vocabulary

immigration (im-ih-GRAY-shuhn) the action of coming to live permanently in a foreign country

processed (PRAH-sesd) enduring a series of tasks or tests

officials (uh-FISH-uhlz) people authorized with power

exclusion (ik-SKLOO-zhuhn) the act of denying access

FLASH FACT!

Much of San Francisco was destroyed after the 1906 earthquake.

Vocabulary

city hall (SIT-ee HAWL) a city government's main building

detained (dih-TAYND) when someone is held back

interrogated (in-TER-uh-gate-id) questioned

deported (dih-PORT-id) when a person is sent back to their native country

In 1906, there was a big fire in San Francisco. It burned down City Hall. All records were lost. Many Chinese workers trying to come to the United States used this to cheat the system. They would pretend to be someone's relative in the United States. They paid these "relatives" a lot of money. They became "paper sons" or "paper daughters." They were only related on paper.

The United States tried to stop this system of fake identities. It detained the Chinese at Angel Island. Other immigrants could go straight to San Francisco, California. But Chinese men and women were separated. They were tested by doctors. They were interrogated for long periods of time. If they failed, they were deported.

CAST of CHARACTERS

NARRATOR: person who helps tell the story

CHEW HOY FONG: 18-year-old Chinese immigrant who is trying to enter the United States as a "paper son"

FEI YEN LEE: wife of a Chinese immigrant who is joining her husband in the United States

SHIP WORKER: a person who works on a ship

DOCTOR: a person who checks the Chinese immigrants for sicknesses

JEAN ANDERSON: a **deaconess** who helps Chinese women and children detained at Angel Island

INTERROGATOR: a person who asks questions to test the Chinese immigrants

Richard Lui was born in the early 1970s. He was born in California. He went to school in San Francisco. He's a journalist and news anchor. He has worked for major news networks. At CNN Worldwide, he was the first Asian American male to anchor a major news show. He's written articles for major newspapers. He also gives a lot of speeches. He's a very successful person. But he has a family secret. He said, "I am the grandson of illegal immigrants. My father's parents came here as paper son and paper daughter. My real last name is Wong, not the name they bought, Lui." Lui's grandparents didn't tell anyone about their secret. They were scared their children and grandchildren would get deported. Their tombstones are the only places with their real names. That's how Lui and his father found out about their history.

Vocabulary
deaconess (DEE-kuhn-es)
a woman who works for a church

FLASH FACT!
The fear of Chinese workers was called "yellow peril."

NARRATOR: **CHEW HOY FONG** *and* **FEI YEN LEE** *are in Hong Kong. They're at a **dock**. There are a lot of people around.*

CHEW: Excuse me? Is this ship going to America?

FEI: Yes, it is. I'm on this ship. Are you also going to America?

CHEW: I am. I hear the streets are **paved** with gold. I need to get work. I need to send money back to my family.

FEI: That sounds like a good plan. Things are so bad here. The wars and floods are terrible.

CHEW: I don't want to leave my family. But I have no choice. It's hard to live here. Our crops are ruined. We're so poor. My father had to sell our farm. We had to borrow money from my uncle. America is our only hope!

Vocabulary
dock (DAHK) place where ships are tied up until they sail off
paved (PAYVD) covered over

FLASH FACT!
Chinese people called California Gam Saan, which means "Gold Mountain."

FEI: Yes, there are more opportunities in America.

CHEW: Is that why you're going there?

FEI: My husband lives in San Francisco. My daughters and I are joining him. He finally sent enough **funds** home to pay for our travel.

CHEW: Lucky you! That's great you know someone over there already. I'm so scared. I don't know anyone.

FEI: You're too young to be alone. You must have some family in America?

CHEW: Well, I guess I have a family. But I don't really know them. You see, I'm a . . .

NARRATOR: *Chew is interrupted by a* **SHIP WORKER**.

SHIP WORKER: All aboard! We're setting sail for the United States of America! All aboard!

FEI: It's time to go. I'll see you on the ship. You can tell me more about yourself later. Nice meeting you!

Vocabulary
funds (FUHNDZ) money

FLASH FACT!
Many Chinese immigrants settled in San Francisco, California. This area became known as Chinatown.

NARRATOR: *It takes 22 days to sail from Hong Kong to Angel Island.* **CHEW HOY FONG** *and* **FEI YEN LEE** *run into each other on the ship.*

CHEW: I see you're reading your **coaching papers**. Are you a paper daughter? I'm a paper son!

FEI: Shhh! Not so loud. You need to be careful. You shouldn't tell anyone you're a paper son.

CHEW: Why not? Aren't we all the same?

FEI: No, we're not the same. Paper sons are **illegally** coming to the United States. I'm doing it the legal way. My husband is a **merchant**. He owns a shop. He's also a **naturalized** citizen. This means he's allowed to bring over his family.

CHEW: It's so hard to immigrate to the United States these days. The Chinese Exclusion Act has been really unfair to the Chinese workers.

LOCATION SHOOTING
REAL-WORLD SETTING

Angel Island is a large island in the San Francisco Bay. It's the perfect place for a detention center. First, there's no escaping. In fact, it's close to Alcatraz. Alcatraz is a famous prison. Second, it's far away from the mainland. Being far kept sick immigrants away from U.S. citizens. Third, the water is really cold. The waves are rough. Sharks swim in the waters. Today, Angel Island is a state park. The immigration station is on the island's northeastern corner. It's now a museum. It's a national historical landmark. This is because of the wall carvings. Chinese immigrants wrote poems on the walls. These walls are an important part of history. They tell the stories of many Chinese immigrants.

Vocabulary

coaching papers (KOHCH-ing PAY-purz) lists of facts for Chinese immigrants to memorize for the interrogations

illegally (ih-LEE-guhl-ee) against the law

merchant (MUR-chuhnt) business owner

naturalized (NACH-ur-uh-lized) made a citizen of a country that one was not born in

FLASH FACT!

Hong Kong is in southeastern China.

FEI: It's also unfair that I have to study these coaching papers. My husband said they test everyone at Angel Island.

CHEW: I heard the interrogations are really tough. They kick people out for making one mistake! My paper father said they're trying to keep the Chinese out. He said I need to study hard. He said I need to say the exact same thing he said.

FEI: Do you know your paper father?

CHEW: No. He's my neighbor's cousin. He owns a shop in the United States. He agreed to pretend to be my father. My father paid him a lot of money. That's why I need to get **landed**. I need to pay back our **debts**.

NARRATOR: *A SHIP WORKER approaches.*

SHIP WORKER: What are you two doing up here? Why aren't you in **steerage**?

Vocabulary

landed (LAND-id) to be allowed to immigrate

debts (DETS) money that is owed

steerage (STEER-ij) the ship's lower deck

FLASH FACT!

Some interrogators questioned immigrants aboard the ships.

FEI: We needed to get some air. The toilets down there are **clogged** again. It made me sick.

CHEW: Yes, the smell is awful. Plus, there's no room to move around.

SHIP WORKER: Okay. Well, we should be at Angel Island soon.

FEI: Thank goodness he's gone. Do you think he saw the coaching papers?

CHEW: I don't think so. But remember to throw them over the ship.

FEI: Why? I haven't even really started studying them yet.

CHEW: My paper father said not to get caught with the coaching papers. If people find them, then we'll get deported right away.

FEI: Okay. Well I hope my answers will be enough.

CHEW: Look ahead! I see land! Good luck to you!

Vocabulary
clogged (KLAHGD) stopped up

FLASH FACT!
The Angel Island Immigration Station was known as China Cove. It was built for controlling Chinese entry into the United States.

NARRATOR: *The Chinese immigrants are put into **ferry** boats. They are taken to Angel Island. The men and women are separated. They're taken to see a doctor.* **CHEW HOY FONG** *is being examined by a* **DOCTOR***.*

CHEW: Why do we need to do this?

DOCTOR: We need to make sure you're not sick. We don't want you to bring sicknesses into the country. We do this to protect our citizens.

CHEW: I'm healthy. I didn't even get seasick.

DOCTOR: It doesn't matter what you say. I still need to check you. Please use this bowl.

CHEW: What do I do with it?

DOCTOR: Go to the bathroom in it. I need to check your **stool**. You could have worms.

CHEW: I'm not sick. What if I don't do it?

DOCTOR: Then you'll be deported.

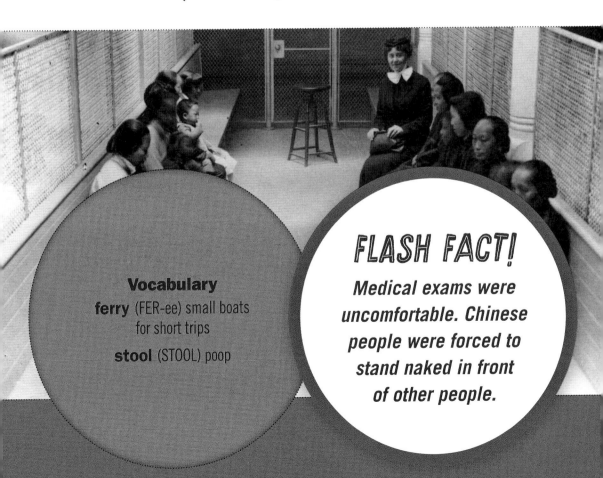

Vocabulary
ferry (FER-ee) small boats for short trips
stool (STOOL) poop

FLASH FACT!
Medical exams were uncomfortable. Chinese people were forced to stand naked in front of other people.

NARRATOR: *After the medical exams, the Chinese immigrants are taken to their* **dorms.** *In the women's dorms,* **JEAN ANDERSON** *is there. She helps* **FEI YEN LEE** *get settled.*

Vocabulary
dorms (DORMZ) buildings with bedrooms

FLASH FACT!
The longest recorded stay at Angel Island was 22 months.

FEI: This can't be where we sleep! There's hardly any room. The beds are so close together. They're also stacked on top of each other. And there are bars on the windows. It's like we're in jail!

JEAN: I know, dear. It's just awful. We must make do. Hopefully, you'll be landed soon.

FEI: Look at these poems on the walls. People are writing about their lives here. Some say they've been detained for months. Months? There's nothing to do here!

JEAN: We must keep our minds busy. I brought you some games, music, and books.

FEI: The books are in English. I can't read English.

JEAN: I'll teach you.

FEI: Why do you help us, Jean?

JEAN: God teaches us to serve all those in need. The government has not treated the Chinese well. But not all my friends and family feel the same way I do. My brother-in-law is out of work. He blames the Chinese for stealing his job. I don't agree with him. I think we all want the same thing. We want better lives.

NARRATOR: *Chinese immigrants are interrogated for a long time. Interrogators are trying to trick the immigrants. They want to catch them in lies. There's also an **interpreter** in the room.* **CHEW HOY FONG** *waited 3 weeks for his **hearing**. He was interrogated every day for 2 weeks by his* **INTERROGATOR**.

INTERROGATOR: How many windows are in your house in China?

Vocabulary

interpreter (in-TUR-prit-ur) a person who translates what someone says in one language to another language

hearing (HEER-ing) opportunity to state one's case

FLASH FACT!

At Angel Island, the Chinese immigrants could only go outside for a little bit each morning. They were locked in every night.

CHEW: I think 3. No, 5.

INTERROGATOR: You're not sure?

CHEW: I'm sorry. I'm nervous and tired. There are 3 doors. And 5 windows.

INTERROGATOR: Where is the rice bin?

CHEW: On the right side of the kitchen door.

INTERROGATOR: Where do you sleep?

CHEW: In the bedroom I share with my cousin.

INTERROGATOR: How many chickens do you have?

CHEW: I have 14 chickens. You've been interrogating me for a long time. When will I be landed?

INTERROGATOR: You've answered all the questions correctly. Your answers match your father's answers. So, we will approve you. Welcome to the United States!

NARRATOR: FEI YEN LEE *was also interrogated. But she did not pass. She is comforted by* **JEAN ANDERSON**.

FEI: Oh, Jean! They're going to deport me and my daughters! They said I made too many mistakes. They said my daughters didn't answer any of the questions correctly.

JEAN: For goodness' sake! They're just little girls. This is a **discriminating** process. The government isn't interrogating any other group. They're just targeting the Chinese. I'm so sorry this is happening to you.

BLOOPERS
HISTORICAL MISTAKES

During World War II, the United States was at war against Japan. China became a U.S. ally. In 1943, President Franklin D. Roosevelt made a speech. He said, "Nations, like individuals, make mistakes. We must be big enough to acknowledge our mistakes of the past and to correct them. By the repeal of the Chinese exclusion laws, we can correct a historic mistake." The Chinese Exclusion Act of 1882 restricted the immigration of Chinese people. It denied Chinese people the right to become citizens. The act was inspired by fear. White workers were worried. Chinese workers worked for less pay. White workers blamed the Chinese for lowering wages. They blamed them for taking away jobs. Many think the Chinese exclusion laws were racist. In 2012, the U.S. Congress apologized for passing these laws.

Vocabulary

discriminating (dis-KRIM-uh-nate-ing) treating people differently in a bad way

FLASH FACT!

Some of the Chinese men formed a special group called Zizhihui. This means the Angel Island Liberty Association. They helped each other get through the days.

27

FEI: They asked such silly questions. I have no idea where my neighbor's rice bin is. I don't know how many houseplants we have. Do you know these things?

JEAN: I do not. The questions do seem unfair.

FEI: I am the wife of a Chinese merchant. My daughters are the children of a Chinese merchant. We have not lied. We have the right papers. Why am I being punished? I just want to be with my husband. I want to be a family again.

JEAN: We must not give up. I will write letters to the government. We must get people's attention.

FEI: I was able to contact my husband. He said he has a lawyer. He's going to **appeal** the ruling. We're going to fight.

JEAN: That's good.

FEI: But all we can do now is wait and hope.

本屋拘留幾次

解困墨例致意

只聽英雄未

可惜英雄無

各位鄉君眾

從今遠別此

莫道其間君

誘感王勳爰

Vocabulary
appeal (uh-PEEL) to apply
for a reversal of a decision

FLASH FACT!

*Many of the poems
written on the walls
of Angel Island
still exist.*

EVENT TIMELINE

January 24, 1848: Gold is discovered in California. The Gold Rush begins. Chinese people start coming to the United States. They want to make money to send back home.

February 1848: The first Chinese immigrants to California arrive in San Francisco. Two men and a woman come from Hong Kong. They sail on the *Eagle*.

April 13, 1850: California passes the Foreign Miners Tax. This law forces Chinese workers to pay a lot of money to work. Many Chinese quit. The law was repealed in 1851.

1850s–1930s: There are wars and floods in China. Many Chinese flee to the United States. They need money. They hope for better lives.

January 20, 1865: Charles Crocker owned a railroad company. He hires Chinese immigrants to build the transcontinental railroad.

October 1, 1875: The U.S. Supreme Court rules that the federal government, not states, is in charge of immigration policies. The case is known as *Chy Lung vs. Freeman*.

May 6, 1882: The United States passes the Chinese Exclusion Act. This stops Chinese workers from immigrating.

May 5, 1892: The Geary Act extends the Chinese Exclusion Act. It requires Chinese people to carry permits. Without their permits, they could be deported.

July 20, 1905: The Chinese Boycott begins. A Chinese group in San Francisco pushes China to pressure the United States to treat them better. Cities in China stop buying U.S. goods. The boycott lasts about a year.

April 18, 1906: An earthquake hits San Francisco. There's a great fire that lasts several days. All immigration records are destroyed.

January 21, 1910: The Angel Island Immigration Station opens. About 18 percent of immigrants are deported.

November 5, 1940: The U.S. government closes the Angel Island Immigration Station.

December 17, 1943: The United States passes the Magnuson Act. This repeals the Chinese exclusion laws.

CONSIDER THIS!

TAKE A POSITION! What are the pros and cons of having immigration policies? Do you think the United States was right or wrong in the handling of Chinese immigrants at Angel Island? Argue your point with reasons and evidence.

SAY WHAT? Explain the immigration process. Describe what the Chinese immigrants had to go through. Compare their experience to what is happening today. How have things changed? How have they stayed the same?

THINK ABOUT IT! Learn more about what it means to be a paper son or paper daughter. Would you be willing to be a paper son or paper daughter? Why or why not? What would be the risks for you? What would be the benefits?

Learn More

Brimner, Larry Dane. *Angel Island.* New York, NY: Children's Press, 2001.

Freedman, Russell. *Angel Island: Gateway to Gold Mountain.* New York, NY: Clarion Books, 2013.

James, Helen Foster, and Virginia Shin-Mui Loh. *Paper Son: Lee's Journey to America.* Ann Arbor, MI: Sleeping Bear Press, 2013.

Kallio, Jamie. *Angel Island Immigration.* Ann Arbor, MI: Cherry Lake Publishing, 2015.

Lee, Milly, and Yangsook Choi (illustr.). *Landed.* New York, NY: Farrar, Straus, and Giroux, 2006.

Yep, Laurence, with Kathleen S. Yep. *The Dragon's Child: A Story of Angel Island.* New York, NY: HarperCollins, 2008.

INDEX

ABOUT THE AUTHOR

Dr. Virginia Loh-Hagan is an author, university professor, and former classroom teacher. She is the co-author of *Paper Son: Lee's Journey to America*, which was nominated for a California Young Reader Medal award. She's also visited Angel Island and highly recommends the experience. She lives in San Diego with her very tall husband and very naughty dogs. To learn more about her, visit www.virginialoh.com.